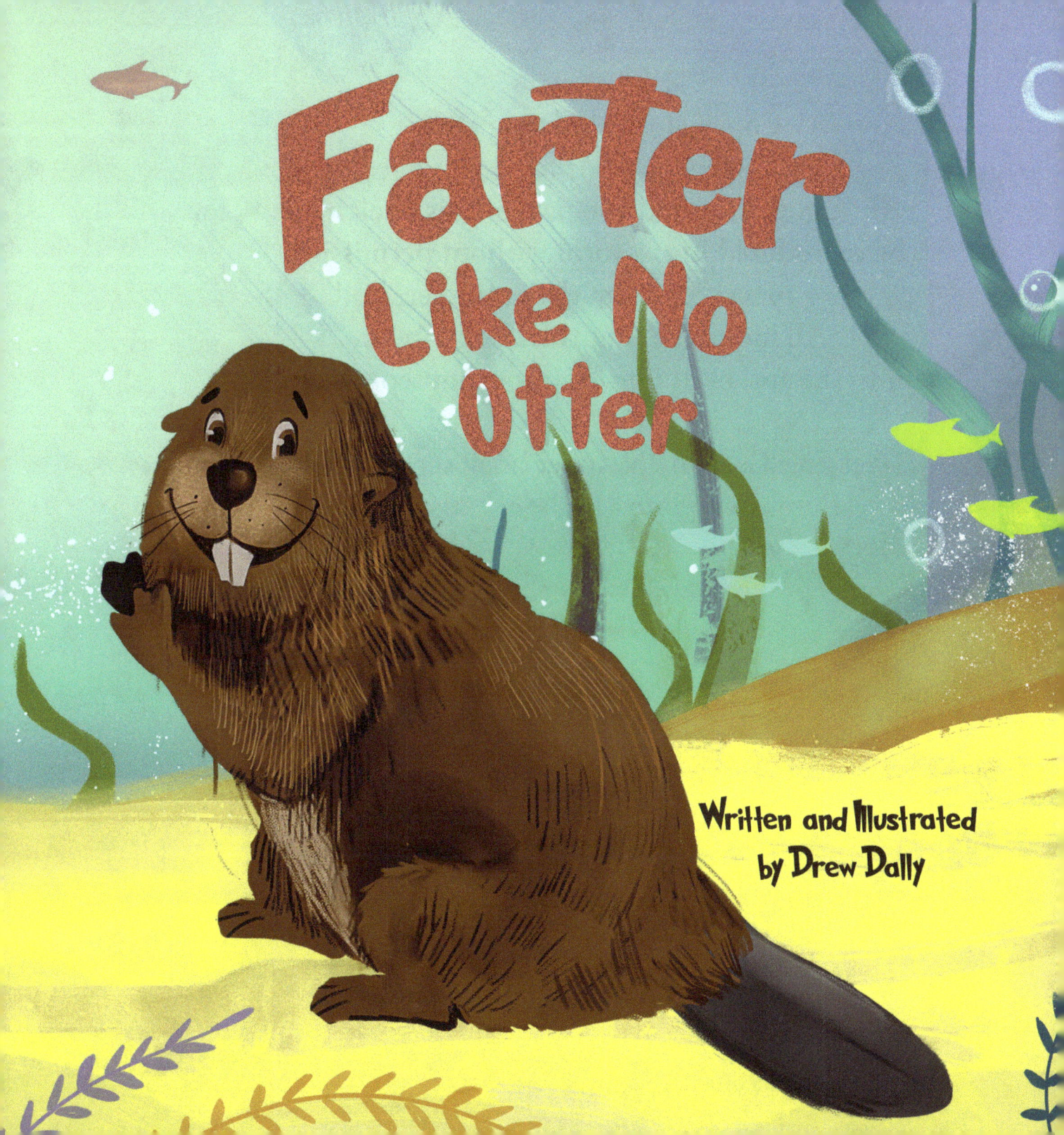

Copyright 2023 Drew Dally

ISBN: 978-1-961443-13-6

All Rights Reserved. No part of this book may be reproduced in any form without permission in writing from the publisher.
All inquires about this book can be sent to the author at info@harbourhousepress.co.uk

Get Free Color by Number book send a Mail After Purchase to info@harbourhousepress.co.uk

Dedicated to my Sons:
Videl, Vishal & Valen

Harbour
HOUSE PUBLISHING LTD

In a cozy little river near the town of Splotter,
Lived an otter who could "Farter Like No Otter."
His name was Ollie, and he was a sight,
For when he would fart, the fish would take flight.

He'd wiggle his tail, and then with a grin,
he'd let out a toot that would make the reeds spin.

He could poot like a piccolo, rumble like a drum, and sometimes, his farts would even hum.

The critters would gather, from far and wide, to listen and laugh at Ollie's rear side.

One sunny day, as the pups played by the shore, Ollie decided it was time to fart even more.

He tooted and tooted, and the water did splash, and each time he did, the critters would gasp.

The animals gathered, as they heard the commotion, and they couldn't believe the sounds of devotion.

So he declared a special day, right there and then, a "Farter's Day" celebration to happen again.

Each year, the otters would gather and toot, and the critters would laugh, and the fish would scoot.

As the years went by, the tradition did grow,
and the laughter and joy continued to flow.
The cozy little river thrived by Splotter,
As they celebrated Ollie, the "Farter Like No Otter."

So remember the otter who could fart like no other,
And let his story live on, through sister and brother.
For laughter and love, they make life worthwhile,
And a funny farting otter can always bring a smile.

# The End.
# Here is Your Free Gift

GET THIS BOOK
FREE NOW

→

Scan This Code
or Visit >>

bit.ly/Einkling

Printed in the USA
CPSIA information can be obtained
at www.ICGtesting.com
LVHW012122041123
762867LV00006B/48